NATIONAL GEOGRAPHIC

AMERICAN DOCUMENTS

The Mayflower Compact

Pilgrims

Judith Lloyd Yero

Picture Credits

Cover (flag) Getty Images; cover (document) sail1620.org; cover (ship), 9, 12 (top and bottom), 13 (bottom), 15, 16-17, 22, 23, 24 (right and bottom) Bettmann/Corbis; page 1 Lake County Museum/Corbis; pages 2-3, 14-15, 26-27 Burstein Collection/Corbis; page 4 AP Wide World Photos; pages 4-5, 8 Mary Evans Picture Library; page 10 National Gallery Collection, by kind permission of the National Gallery, London/Corbis; page 11 (top) Kevin Fleming/Corbis; pages 11 (bottom), 17, 18, 24 (middle), 25 Hulton | Archive/Getty Images; page 13 (top) Peter Harholdt/Corbis; pages 20-21 Museum of the City of New York/Corbis; page 21 Brooks Kraft/Corbis; pages 24 (left), 30 Royalty-Free/Corbis; page 28 David Samuel Robbins/Corbis; page 29 Geoffrey Clements/Corbis; page 31 Ed Young/Corbis.

Produced through the worldwide resources of the National Geographic Society, John M. Fahey, Jr., President and Chief Executive Officer; Gilbert M. Grosvenor, Chairman of the Board; Nina D. Hoffman, Executive Vice President and President, Books and Education Publishing Group.

Prepared by National Geographic School Publishing and Children s Books

Ericka Markman, Senior Vice President and President, Children's Books and Education Publishing Group; Steve Mico, Vice President, Editorial Director; Marianne Hiland, Executive Editor; Anita Schwartz, Project Editor, Suzanne Patrick Fonda, Children's Books Project Editor; Jim Hiscott, Design Manager; Kristin Hanneman, Illustrations Manager; Diana Bourdrez, Picture Editor; Matt Wascavage, Manager of Publishing Services; Sean Philpotts, Production Manager; Jane Ponton, Production Artist.

Manufacturing and Quality Management

Christopher A. Liedel, Chief Financial Officer; Phillip L. Schlosser, Director; Clifton M. Brown III, Manager.

Consultants/Reviewers

Dr. Paul Finkelman, Chapman Distinguished Professor of Law, University of Tulsa Law School, Tulsa, Oklahoma

Dr. Margit E. McGuire, School of Education, Seattle University, Seattle, Washington

Book Development

Nieman Inc.

Book Design

Steven Curtis Design, Inc.

Art Direction

Dan Banks, Project Design Company

Photo Research

Corrine L. Brock, In the Lupe, Inc.

ISBN 0-7922-5891-6 (hardcover)

ISBN 0-7922-5892-4 (library binding)

Previously published as *Documents of Freedom: The Mayflower Compact* (National Geographic Reading Expeditions). Copyright © 2004; ISBN 0-7922-4553-9 (paperback)

Published by the NATIONAL GEOGRAPHIC SOCIETY
1145 17th Street, N.W.
Washington, D.C. 20036-4688

Printed in the U.S.A.

Table of Contents

Introduction

I magine you and your family are leaving your home forever. You travel in a small sailboat with some other people across 3,000 miles of ocean. The trip is scary, and at times you are not sure you will make it. When you finally land, you see only forests. No buildings or roads have been built yet.

The *Mayflower* passengers braved a long journey to America to seek religious freedom for themselves.

No houses or soft beds wait for you. No cozy inn will give you a hot meal. It is winter. The little food you have brought with you is nearly gone, and you will have to figure out where to find more.

What would you do first? The men, women, and children who sailed on the *Mayflower* must have wondered the same thing. Everyone would have to pull together if the group was to survive. How would they agree on the rules for their new society? Who would be in charge?

In 1620, this group of **colonists** arrived in the area of Cape Cod, Massachusetts. Before they ever set foot on shore, they wrote and signed an agreement called the Mayflower Compact. This famous document helped establish democracy in North America. Here is their story and their document of freedom.

Many New England towns hold town meetings in the tradition the *Mayflower* colonists began.

On Display

We know about the Mayflower Compact from the Plymouth Colony's governor, William Bradford. The original document no longer exists. The copy shown here is from Bradford's handwritten book, *Of Plimoth Plantation*.

The Ship

The *Mayflower* was supposed to return home after dropping off the colonists. Christopher Jones, the captain, decided to stay through the first winter. If he had not, the settlers would have had no shelter, and the Plymouth Colony probably wouldn't have survived. The ship returned to England in May of 1621. It was never again used to carry passengers.

Age

The average age of the men was 34. William Brewster was one of the oldest—about 53. John Carver, the first governor, was 44, and William Bradford was 30 when the *Mayflower* landed.

The Signers

Forty-one men signed the Compact. Each man signed for his whole family, including the women, younger men, children, and servants. Several men on board were sick and did not sign.

...do by these presents, solemnly & mutually in the presence of God and one of another, covenant and combine ourselves together into a civil body politick...

Plymouth Colony reconstruction

sett by them done (this their condition considered) might
be as firme as any patent; and in some respects more sure.
The forme was as followeth.

In y̆ name of god Amen. We whose names are underwriten,
the loyall subjects of our dread soueraigne Lord king James
by y̆ grace of god, of great Britaine, franc, & Ireland king,
defender of y̆ faith, &c.

Haueing undertaken, for y̆ glorie of god, and aduancemente
of y̆ christian faith, and honour of our king & countrie, a voyage to
plant y̆ first colonie in y̆ Northerne parts of Virginia. doe
by these presents solemnly & mutualy in y̆ presence of god, and
one of another, couenant, & combine our selues togeather into a
ciuill body politick, for our better ordering, & preseruation & fur=
therance of y̆ ends aforsaid; and by vertue hearof to enacte,
constitute, and frame shuch just & equall lawes, ordinances,
Acts, constitutions, & offices, from time to time, as shall be thought
most meete & conuenient for y̆ generall good of y̆ colonie: unto
which we promise all due submission and obedience. In witnes
wherof we haue hereunder subscribed our names at Cap=
Codd y̆ .11. of Nouember, in y̆ year of y̆ raigne of our soueraigne
Lord king James of England, france, & Ireland y̆ eighteenth
and of Scotland y̆ fiftie fourth. An̄: Dom. 1620.|

After this they chose, or rather confirmed, m̄ John Caruer (a man
godly & well approued amongst them) their Gouernour for that
year. And after they had prouided a place for their goods, or
comone store, (which were long in unlading, for want of boats,
foulnes of y̆ winter weather, and sicknes of diuers) and begune
some small cottages for their habitation; as time would admite
they mette and consulted of lawes, & orders, both for their
ciuill, & military gouernmente, as y̆ necessitie of their condi=
tion did require, still adding therunto as urgent occasion
in seuerall times, and in cases did require.

In these hard & difficulte beginings they found some discontents
& murmurings amongst some, arise and mutinous speeches & cariags
in other; but they were soone quelled, & ouercome, by y̆ wis=
dome, patience, and y̆ just & equall carrage of things, by y̆ gou̅r
and better part w̄ch clane faithfully togeather in y̆ maine.
But that which was most sadd, & lamentable, was, that in 2.
or .3. monoths time halfe of their company dyed, especialy
in Jan: & february, being y̆ depth of winter, and wanting
houses & other comforts; being infected with y̆ scuruie &

Early Colonists

Who were the people we know today as the Pilgrims?
Why did they come to America?

★

Religious Freedom

In the 1600s, kings and queens of England weren't the only ones who wore fancy robes and jeweled crowns. Bishops—the leaders of the **Church of England**—also dressed like royalty. The Church of England was the official religion of the country.

Some Christian people in England wanted to worship God in a different way. They did not want a fancy church with altars, candles, and pipe organs. They wanted good men as their church leaders—not rich ones. We do not need priests to stand between us and God, they said. We can pray to Him ourselves.

The **Separatists** believed it was impossible to change the Church of England, so they decided to separate from it. They formed their own churches.

Some people mocked the Separatists' habits.

One Separatist group began in Scrooby, a small town in northern England. The people met in the home of William Brewster, the town's postmaster. They elected men, called **elders,** to run their church, and they hired a preacher. Like the saints in the holy stories, they tried to live good lives. They even called themselves "saints." Other people in Scrooby made fun of them. They refused to buy the farm produce from the Separatists. Shopkeepers even refused to sell them supplies.

The king, James I, was angry too. Who were these people to go about electing their leaders? What would happen to the power of the king or the bishops if these so-called "saints" got their way? It was unthinkable! King James ordered some of the Separatists arrested.

The Separatists decided to leave England. They knew that in Holland the Dutch let people worship as they wished. They also knew they could never get the king's permission to leave. So, they decided to sneak out of the country.

The Separatists sold their farmland and their homes. They took only what they could carry. In the dark of night, they slipped out of Scrooby.

William Brewster

William Brewster was a man of the world. He had gone to a university. He read Latin and Greek. He had worked for England's queen. The Separatists in Scrooby listened to him and elected him an elder in their new church. His money helped them escape from England.

Life Among the Dutch

Trouble followed trouble as the Scrooby group tried to leave England. One ship's captain took their money and then turned them over to the authorities. Another left the women and children on shore because he was afraid to stay in port too long. The Separatists sold some of the little they had and tried again.

By 1609, most of the group, along with Separatists from other parts of England, had settled in the Dutch city of Leiden (LYD–uhn). There they signed a **covenant**—an agreement to form their own church. The Separatists enjoyed the religious freedom of Holland. In other ways, however, life was harder than it had been at home.

In England, most of the Separatists had been farmers. In Holland, farmland near Leiden was very expensive. The Separatists did not have enough money left to buy land. So, they had to look for other work. Dutch workers in Leiden spun and dyed yarn and then wove it into beautiful cloth. The Separatists were not trained in this kind of work. They had to take the lowest paying jobs. They barely had enough to live on.

The Separatists had one another, but they were living among strangers. The children learned the Dutch language. The parents worried because their children behaved more like Dutch than like English children.

After a few years, the Separatists decided they had to leave. They did not want to return to England. Where could they go? South America had warm weather and rich farmland. The Separatists decided that the heat would not suit their "English bodies." In North America, English people had settled in the Virginia Colony. They would try to go there.

Spinning and weaving supplies

William Bradford

William Bradford was about 17 when he joined the Scrooby group. His parents had died when he was nine. His aunts and uncles ordered him to stay away from the saints. Instead, he went to live with William Brewster, who treated him like a son. William Bradford grew to become a Pilgrim leader. He helped organize the *Mayflower* trip to America.

Preparation for the Journey

It would be expensive to travel to North America. For money, the Separatist leaders turned to the Virginia Company. This group of London investors had a **charter,** a grant from the king to help settle and manage the English colony in America, which was called Virginia. A sponsor was found to pay for the trip to America.

This time they would not be running away, as they did when they went to Holland. The Separatists would be going with the blessing of the king. To the king, his subjects were resources. He did not want them working for the Dutch. If they were willing to help settle an English colony, that was useful to him.

Some church members were afraid of the long journey. In the end, fewer than 40 Separatists planned to go. The people who paid for the trip knew that harsh life in the American colony took many lives. To make sure their plan succeeded, they signed up other English people. These people did not all share the Separatists' religion, but they did want a better life. The Separatists called these people "the Strangers."

The seal of the Virginia Colony

Next, the Separatists hired Myles Standish and John Alden. Captain Standish was a professional soldier. He would take charge of defending the new colony. Alden was a **cooper,** or barrel maker. Barrels were needed to store all kinds of supplies.

John Alden

John Alden was a tall, blond, blue-eyed man barely out of his teens. He agreed to go to America for one year. While there, he would build the barrels in which the colonists shipped goods back to England. When the year was over, Alden chose to stay. He married Priscilla Mullens, the daughter of another colonist, and became a leader in the colony.

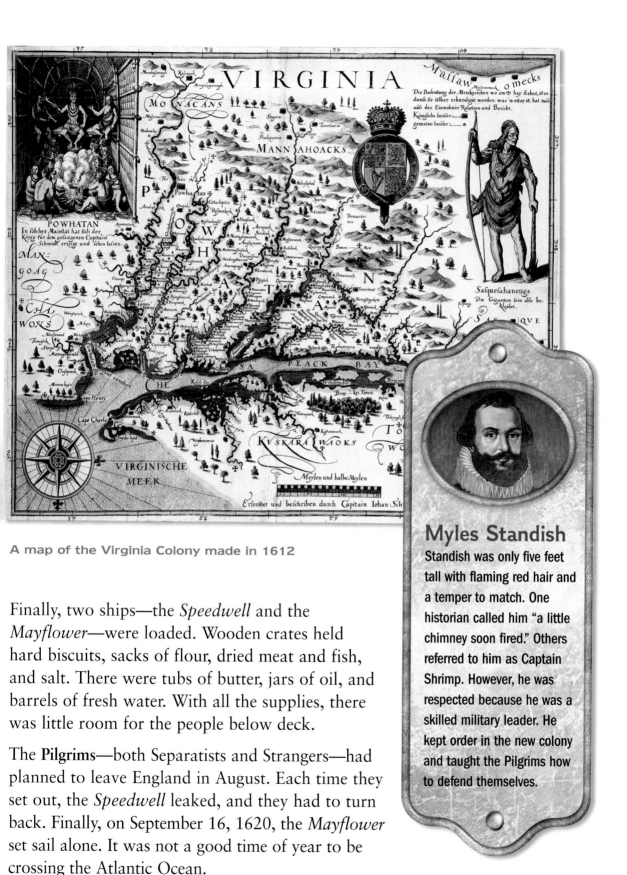

A map of the Virginia Colony made in 1612

Finally, two ships—the *Speedwell* and the *Mayflower*—were loaded. Wooden crates held hard biscuits, sacks of flour, dried meat and fish, and salt. There were tubs of butter, jars of oil, and barrels of fresh water. With all the supplies, there was little room for the people below deck.

The **Pilgrims**—both Separatists and Strangers—had planned to leave England in August. Each time they set out, the *Speedwell* leaked, and they had to turn back. Finally, on September 16, 1620, the *Mayflower* set sail alone. It was not a good time of year to be crossing the Atlantic Ocean.

Myles Standish

Standish was only five feet tall with flaming red hair and a temper to match. One historian called him "a little chimney soon fired." Others referred to him as Captain Shrimp. However, he was respected because he was a skilled military leader. He kept order in the new colony and taught the Pilgrims how to defend themselves.

Voyage of the *Mayflower*

The voyage started peacefully, with sunny skies and light winds. Still, the ship pitched and rolled with the ocean's waves. The passengers became seasick. The sailors were not used to having passengers. They made fun of them, calling them "glib-glabbety puke-stockings."

One especially nasty sailor said the travelers would die. He swore he would laugh when their bodies were thrown overboard. After two weeks at sea, however, he became ill and died. *His* was the body thrown overboard! Other sailors wondered, was the Pilgrims' God responsible? After this event, they treated their passengers with respect.

The ship was crowded. More than 30 sailors and 102 passengers were crammed into a space about the size of a basketball court. The Pilgrims slept among chests filled with blankets and clothes and small pieces of furniture. Crates held axes for cutting down trees and hoes for digging. The ship had no heat. The only fire was in an iron box filled with sand. People took turns heating food. Most people ate their salted fish and meat cold, along with rock-hard biscuits.

With 34 children and 2 dogs, the sailors' tempers flared. Passenger John Howland fell overboard. He grabbed a trailing rope and held on until he was pulled in. Storms raged. The main beams of the ship cracked. In mid-ocean, Elizabeth Hopkins gave birth to a son.

One passenger died. Others became ill from the poor diet and harsh conditions. If they did not reach land soon, they might all be dead.

Finally, after 66 days at sea, Pilgrims heard the cry, "Land ho!" This land, however, was not in the Virginia Colony. A storm had blown them several hundred miles north. Seeking Virginia, they sailed south. Another storm blew them out to sea. They had no desire to keep sailing. On November 10, 1620, the *Mayflower* anchored off Cape Cod.

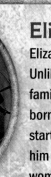

Elizabeth Hopkins

Elizabeth Hopkins traveled with her husband Stephen. Unlike some other men, he was not afraid to bring his family. The baby they were expecting should have been born in America. Because the voyage got such a late start, the Hopkins's son was born at sea. They named him Oceanus. Elizabeth Hopkins was one of only four women who survived the first winter in America.

Writing and Signing the Mayflower Compact

Before any passengers left the *Mayflower,* they had one problem to solve. The Virginia Company agreement was for a settlement in territory under English rule. They had not landed in that territory. Because of this, some Strangers in the group claimed the agreement was broken. Some of the younger men threatened to leave the group once they landed.

The Separatists knew they had strength and safety in numbers. Winter was near. They had settled in an unknown land with unknown dangers. They needed the Strangers— they needed *everyone*—if the colony was to survive. They needed an agreement for governing their settlement that everyone would accept. They needed it now!

Two leaders were chosen to write the **compact.** William Brewster represented the Separatists. Stephen Hopkins was the leader of the Strangers.

Signatures of some of the signers

Signing the Mayflower Compact aboard ship

They were both well educated and shared English ideas about government. They knew what a document about a community's government should say.

On November 11, 1620, the Mayflower Compact was signed. Their work done, the men hurried out on deck to see their new home. William Bradford later told how he felt in that moment. The land looked "wild and savage." The great ocean separated the Pilgrims from everything they knew. No friends or family welcomed them. They were tired and weak, and they faced the task of building homes and finding food. Yet, they had faith that God would take care of them.

"when they came ashore they would use their own liberty, for none had power to command them"

This, wrote Bradford, is what the Strangers said they would do. Their "discontented and mutinous" talk was the reason for the Mayflower Compact.

A Closer Look

In fewer than 200 words, the Mayflower Compact laid the groundwork for democracy in America.

★

Authority and Law

The men who wrote the Mayflower Compact built their agreement on a firm foundation. They began by calling on God. Next, they said that they were loyal subjects of King James. They were not setting up a new country. They recognized the authority that both God and the king had over them.

Yet, they needed a government and laws. If they were in Virginia, their laws would come from the Virginia Company. In this northern part of America, there was no law they recognized. So, this is what they wrote.

The Pilgrims walk to church in the snow.

What it means	What they wrote
We, the loyal subjects of King James,	*In the name of God, Amen. We whose names are underwritten, the loyal subjects of our dread sovereign lord, King James, by the grace of God, of Great Britain, France, and Ireland king, defender of the faith, etc.*
have for religious reasons	*Having undertaken, for the glory of God and advancement of the Christian faith*
and for our nation's reasons,	*and honor of our king & country,*
traveled to start the first colony in the northern part of Virginia.	*a voyage to plant the first colony in the Northern parts of Virginia,*
In front of each other and God,	*do by these presents, solemnly & mutually in the presence of God and one of another,*
we come together to form a government	*covenant & combine ourselves together into a civil body politick,*
so we can meet our goals	*for our better ordering & preservation & furtherance of the ends foresaid:*
and make laws and create officials	*and by virtue hereof to enact laws, ordinances, acts, constitutions, & offices,*
when we need to, for the good of the whole colony.	*from time to time, as shall be thought most meet & convenient for the general good of the Colony,*
We will respect this government and its laws.	*unto which we promise all due submission and obedience*

In witness whereof we have hereunder subscribed our names at Cape Cod the 11th of November in the year of the reign of our sovereign lord, King James, of England, France, & Ireland the eighteenth and of Scotland, the fifty-fourth. Ano: Dom. 1620.

Who Needs Rules?

Would it be great to live in a land without rules? Suppose you and your schoolmates have been forced to move everything to a new school. No one is in charge! People are running all over the place. Some students do a lot of work, and others sit around doing nothing. Important things have been left behind. No one remembered to order food for the cafeteria. Who has the keys to open the building? What a mess!

Arriving at Plymouth

20

For any community to be successful, someone has to be in charge. The *Mayflower* group knew this. The Pilgrims had a lot of work to do. What should be done first? Who should do it? Decisions like these had to be made. Everyone in the group needed to agree to go along with the plans the leaders made.

For the Separatists, the Compact served the same purpose as the agreement they made when they formed a Separatist church. They wrote an agreement to work together. They elected leaders and promised one another that they would do what the leaders decided.

The Strangers understood the need for government. They liked the idea of a government that they could choose. So, they were willing to go along with the idea. Their new colony would have a governor and laws. They could get on with the work of building new lives.

Pilgrims and Presidents

What if John Howland had not been rescued when he fell overboard? Several U.S. Presidents might never have been born! George Bush, and George W. Bush are both descendants of John Howland. At least six other Presidents were related to *Mayflower* passengers. They include John Adams, John Quincy Adams, Ulysses S. Grant, and Franklin D. Roosevelt.

Living with the Mayflower Compact

The first winter was terrible, but the little colony survived. Law and order kept the community working. Their faith kept the Pilgrims strong.

★

The First Winter

After the men of the *Mayflower* signed the Mayflower Compact, they elected Pilgrim John Carver as governor. Then, they went about finding a place to settle. It was November, and winter weather had begun.

The Pilgrims pray for an end to the harsh winter.

Myles Standish led one of the search parties. They were looking for a safe harbor in a place they could easily defend. They needed a source of fresh water and good soil for the crops they would plant in the spring.

The remaining passengers stayed aboard the *Mayflower*. It was a difficult time for everyone. Food was hard to find. The Pilgrims had no way to stay warm or dry. Often, their wet clothing froze from the high winds and icy temperatures. More and more people got sick. The situation grew desperate.

In mid-December, the men found a clearing surrounded by old cornfields. It had everything they needed. Captain Jones sailed the *Mayflower* into the snug harbor nearby. The Pilgrims named their settlement "New Plymouth."

In late December, 1620, the men started work on their first building—a **common house.** So many people were sick, the work went very slowly. At one time, only seven people were healthy enough to take care of everyone else. They made food and nursed the sick people. They buried the people who died during the night in graves without markers. They did not want the Wampanoag Indians who lived in the area to know how few of them were left.

Fifty of the 102 colonists who had come from England died during the next few months. All but four of the women died. Whole families were gone. Most surviving children lost at least one, if not both, of their parents. Other families had to take them in.

During that hard winter, few people challenged John Carver's leadership. Everyone simply tried to stay alive.

Suzanna White

Suzanna enjoyed two "firsts" in the Plymouth Colony. Her son, Peregrine, was the first white baby born in Plymouth. After her husband died, she married Edward Winslow, whose wife had also died. Theirs was the first marriage in the Plymouth Colony.

Native Americans

Samoset

Samoset learned English from fishermen who crossed the ocean each year for cod. He explained the abandoned cornfields and clearing to the Pilgrims. A terrible disease had killed the Patuxet people who had lived there. Today, we believe it must have been a European disease, such as measles or smallpox, for which the Native Americans had no immunity.

Squanto (Tisquantum)

As a young man, Squanto and several other Patuxets had been captured by an Englishman. They were taken to Spain to be sold as slaves. Squanto escaped and spent several years in England. When he returned to America, he found that he was the last member of his tribe.

Massasoit (Ousamequin)

On March 22, 1621, Massasoit signed a peace treaty with the Pilgrims. In it, the Pilgrims and the Indians agreed not to harm each other's people and to come to each other's aid if either was unjustly attacked. The treaty was kept all through Massasoit's lifetime. He died in 1661.

Unexpected Help

March brought hope. The wind shifted, and the sun shone. Though weak, the people began planting seeds in their gardens. One morning, a young Indian named Samoset walked out of the woods and into the village. Raising his hand, the Native American said, "Welcome, Englishmen." Imagine the Pilgrims' surprise! They greeted Samoset and gave him a few gifts. He promised to send someone who spoke better English.

A week later, Squanto arrived. He told the settlers that the land they had settled was once his village. Squanto stayed with the colonists. He taught them how to catch eels and fertilize their fields with fish. He showed them where to find berries, nuts, and plants that were good to eat. He taught them how to grow corn. Later, the Wampanoag chief, Massasoit, arrived in the village. Squanto helped him and the Pilgrim leaders understand one another. They agreed to trade and to live in peace.

Through the summer, more houses were built. Myles Standish trained the men to defend the village if necessary. Everyone worked in the fields. By fall, acres of corn had been harvested. Carrots, turnips, onions, and other vegetables grew in the settlers' gardens. They had plenty of fish, as well as wild birds and animals to hunt.

Squanto shows Myles Standish (in armor) and others around Massachusetts Bay.

The First Thanksgiving

The time had come to celebrate the harvest. The colonists invited the Native Americans to join them, and 90 Indians arrived. The harvest celebration was a three-day party, complete with games and wine made from local grapes. Between meals, young men from among the colonists and the Native Americans ran races and wrestled. They shot at targets—**muskets** against bows and arrows. They played an English game called stoolball—much like croquet.

Some of the stories and pictures of that first Thanksgiving are not correct. It had no long table as the pictures show. People sat around on chests, rocks, and logs, or ate standing up. The Pilgrims had no turkey. The Indians brought deer. Eels, lobsters, and fish were pulled from the sea. The women prepared vegetables, biscuits, and bread. Local strawberries, plums, and cherries were plentiful. Cranberries grew in the area, but the settlers did not eat them until years later.

Life in Plymouth

The governor of Plymouth, John Carver, died in April 1621. The Pilgrims chose William Bradford for their next governor. He was re-elected 30 times. A few times, people challenged his leadership, but most Pilgrims were satisfied with their government.

For the Pilgrims, religion was an important part of everyday life. Families prayed together. On Sundays, everyone marched to church to the beat of a drum. People who did not go to church would have to pay a fine. No one worked on that day. Most people tried very hard to live a godly life.

Crime and Punishment in Plymouth

Crime	Punishment
Cursing God	Three hours in the stocks
Lying in public	10 shilling fine or two hours in the stocks
Stealing	Repay twice the value of what was stolen, or be publicly whipped.
Gambling with dice or cards	40 shilling fine
Wearing "strange" clothes	50 shilling fine
Failing to attend church	10 shilling fine
Working on Sunday	10 shilling fine
Smoking in any street, barn, or outbuilding	1 shilling fine (2 shillings the second time)

(A shilling might buy a pig or goose.)

The colony was not without problems. Some people were lazy and did not do much work. Others committed crimes. However, most crimes were minor. A few, including murder, were punishable by death. What did the Pilgrims consider a crime? The table above shows a few acts and how they were punished. Stocks, whippings, and fines were the usual punishments.

Plymouth's Troublemakers

John Billington and his wife, Eleanor, had two sons, Francis and John, Jr. While playing "hunter" on board ship, Francis shot his father's gun near a barrel of gunpowder and almost blew up the *Mayflower*! In Plymouth, John Jr. wandered off and was brought back by Indians. In 1630, John Billington shot and killed another man. He was the first person in the colony hanged for murder!

Growth and Change

The Plymouth settlers ran their colony from the time they signed the Mayflower Compact. A year later, word came from King James, making the Plymouth government official. More ships arrived, bringing new settlers. As the colony grew in size, its problems grew as well. Some of the new arrivals were not willing to work as hard as the original settlers did. A few men plotted against Governor Bradford and the other leaders, but the colony nonetheless survived.

In the beginning, people were not allowed to move away from the colony. When it was small, Plymouth needed all its settlers to help each other survive. As more people came, the little clearing near the harbor could not hold them all. More farmers needed more land. Over the years, new colonies grew up. In 1691, the Plymouth Colony became part of the larger Massachusetts Bay Colony.

More settlers arrived and built up the Massachusetts Bay Colony.

The *Mayflower* Legacy

The Pilgrims stand as a symbol for Americans. They were hard workers who were not afraid to take risks for their freedom. They showed that people could successfully govern their own society. This was the way of life Americans claimed in the Declaration of Independence and the Constitution.

The Mayflower Compact planted the seeds of democracy in America. Today, we no longer have one governor who, with just a few other elected officials, makes and enforces the laws. We have a president, senators and representatives from each state, judges, state governors, city mayors, law officers, and many others who work in public office. We choose our government and our leaders. The Mayflower Compact stands as the earliest example of American colonists creating their own form of government. It established self-government among the English colonies and ultimately for the United States of America.

Glossary

charter a grant from a ruler giving certain rights

Church of England the official religion of England; also called the Anglican or Episcopalian Church

colonist a person who settles in a colony, a territory ruled by a distant government

common house a building used for meetings and as a house of worship. Until they built their own homes, several families lived in the common house of Plymouth.

compact a strong, solemn agreement or contract, usually between countries

cooper a person who makes barrels

covenant a solemn agreement or contract, usually among people forming a church or religious organization

elders church leaders or officers; members of the church council who run the church

Mayflower a sailing ship that carried a group of Separatists and other colonists to America in 1620

muskets guns used by the colonists to defend themselves. They had other lighter guns that they used for hunting wild birds.

Pilgrims a name later given to those who traveled aboard the *Mayflower* in 1620 and founded Plymouth County

Separatists a group of people who wanted to separate from the Anglican church to form their own church with simpler services

This rock engraved with the date 1620, sits where the Pilgrims are believed to have landed.

The Mayflower Compact

"In the name of God, Amen. We, whose names are underwritten, the Loyal Subjects of our dread Sovereign Lord, King James, by the Grace of God, of England, France and Ireland, King, Defender of the Faith, e&.

Having undertaken for the Glory of God, and Advancement of the Christian Faith, and the Honour of our King and Country, a voyage to plant the first colony in the northern parts of Virginia; do by these presents, solemnly and mutually in the Presence of God and one of another, covenant and combine ourselves together into a civil Body Politick, for our better Ordering and Preservation, and Furtherance of the Ends aforesaid; And by Virtue hereof to enact, constitute, and frame, such just and equal Laws, Ordinances, Acts, Constitutions and Offices, from time to time, as shall be thought most meet and convenient for the General good of the Colony; unto which we promise all due submission and obedience.

In Witness whereof we have hereunto subscribed our names at Cape Cod the eleventh of November, in the Reign of our Sovereign Lord, King James of England, France and Ireland, the eighteenth, and of Scotland the fifty-fourth. Anno Domini, 1620."

Mr. John Carver
Mr. William Bradford
Mr. Edward Winslow
Mr. William Brewster
Isaac Allerton
Myles Standish
John Alden
John Turner
Francis Eaton
James Chilton
John Craxton
John Billington
Joses Fletcher
John Goodman
Mr. Samuel Fuller
Mr. Christopher Martin
Mr. William Mullins
Mr. William White
Mr. Richard Warren
John Howland
Mr. Steven Hopkins
Digery Priest
Thomas Williams
Gilbert Winslow
Edmund Margesson
Peter Brown
Richard Britteridge
George Soule
Edward Tilly
John Tilly

Francis Cooke
Thomas Rogers
Thomas Tinker
John Ridgdale
Edward Fuller
Richard Clark
Richard Gardiner
Mr. John Allerton
Thomas English
Edward Doten
Edward Liester

Note: Biographical information about the Mayflower's passengers can be found online at http://www.mayflower history.com

Mourt's Relation
A Relation or Journal of the Beginning and Proceeding of the English Plantation Settled at Plymouth

Note: Mourt's Relation *was written by Edward Winslow and William Bradford between November 1620 and November 1621. The title probably comes from the fact that it was first published by George Morton in London, in 1622. The text here is taken from Caleb Johnson's MayflowerHistory.com. The entire document can be downloaded from http://www.mayflowerhistory.com.*

Wednesday, the sixth of September, the winds coming east north east, a fine small gale, we loosed from Plymouth, having been kindly entertained and courteously used by divers friends there dwelling, and after many difficulties in boisterous storms, at length, by God's providence, upon the ninth of November following, by break of the day we espied land which was deemed to be Cape Cod, and so afterward it proved. And the appearance of it much comforted us, especially seeing so goodly a land, and wooded to the brink of the sea. It caused us to rejoice together, and praise God that had given us once again to see land. And thus we made our course south south west, purposing to go to a river ten leagues to the south of the Cape, but at night the wind being contrary, we put round again for the bay of Cape Cod; and upon the 11th of November we came to an anchor in the bay, which is a good harbor and pleasant bay, circled round, except in the entrance which is about four miles over from land to land, compassed about to the very sea with oaks, pines, juniper, sassafras, and other sweet wood; it is a harbor wherein a thousand sail of ships may safely ride: there we relieved ourselves with wood and water, and refreshed our people, which our shallop was fitted to coast the bay, to search for a habitation; there was the greatest store of fowl that ever we saw.

And every day we saw whales playing hard by us, of which in that place, if we had instruments and means to take them, we might have made a very rich return, which to our great grief we wanted. Our master and his mate, and others experienced in fishing, professed we might have made three or four thousand pounds worth of oil; they preferred it before Greenland whale-fishing, and purpose the next winter to fish for whale here. For cod we assayed, but found none, there is good store, no doubt, in their season. Neither got we any fish all the time we lay there, but some few little ones on the shore. We found great mussels, and very fat and full of sea-pearl, but we could not eat them, for they made us all sick that did eat, as well sailors as passengers; they caused to cast and scour, but they were soon well again.

The bay is so round and circling, that before we could come to anchor we went round all the points of the compass. We could not come near the shore by three quarters of an English mile, because of shallow water, which was a great prejudice to us, for our people going on shore were forced to wade a bow shot or two in going a-land, which caused many to get colds and coughs, for it was nigh times freezing cold weather.

This day before we came to harbor, observing some not well affected to unity and concord, but gave some appearance of faction, it was thought good there should be an association and agreement that we should combine together in one body, and to submit to such government and governors as we should by common consent agree to make and choose, and set our hands to this that follows word for word.

See Mayflower Compact, page 32.

The same day, so soon as we could we set ashore 15 or 16 men, well armed, with some to fetch wood, for we had none left; as also to see what the land was, and what inhabitants they could meet with. They found it to be a small neck of land; on this side where we lay is the bay, and the further side the sea; the ground or earth, sand hills, much like the downs in Holland, but much better; the crust of the earth a spit's depth excellent black earth; all wooded with oaks, pines, sassafras, juniper, birch, holly, vines, some ash, walnut; the wood for the most part open and without underwood, fit either to go or ride in; at night our people returned, but found not any person, nor habitation, and laded their boat with juniper, which smelled very sweet and strong and of which we burnt the most part of the time we lay there.

Monday, the 13th of November, we unshipped our shallop and drew her on land, to mend and repair her, having been forced to cut her down in bestowing her betwixt the decks, and she was much opened with the people's lying in her, which kept us long there,

for it was 16 or 17 days before the carpenter had finished her. Our people went on shore to refresh themselves, and our women to wash, as they had great need. But whilst we lay thus still, hoping our shallop would be ready in five or six days at the furthers, but our carpenter made slow work of it, so that some of our people, impatient of delay, desired for our better furtherance to travel by land into the country, which was not without appearance of danger, not having the shallop with them, nor means to carry provision, but on their backs, to see whether it might be fit for us to seat in or no, and the rather because as we sailed into the harbor there seemed to be a river opening itself into the main land; the willingness of the persons was liked, but the thing itself, in regard of the danger, was rather permitted than approved, and so with cautions, directions, and instructions, sixteen men were set out with every man his musket, sword, and corslet, under the conduct of Captain Miles Standish, unto whom was adjoined, for counsel and advice, William Bradford, Stephen Hopkins, and Edward Tilley.

Wednesday, the 15th of November, they were set ashore, and when they had ordered themselves in the order of a single file and marched about the space of a mile, by the sea they espied five or six people with a dog, coming towards them, who were savages, who when they saw them, ran into the wood and whistled the dog after them, etc. First they supposed them to be Master Jones, the master, and some of his men, for they were ashore and knew of their coming, but after they knew them to be Indians they marched after them into the woods, lest other of the Indians should lie in ambush; but when the Indians saw our men following them, they ran away with might and main and our men turned out of the wood after them, for it was the way they intended to go, but they could not come near them. They followed them that night about ten miles by the trace of their footings, and saw how they had come the same way they went, and at a turning perceived how they ran up a hill, to see whether they followed them. At length night came upon them, and they were constrained to take up their lodging, so they set forth three sentinels, and the rest, some kindled a fire, and others fetched wood, and there held our rendezvous that night.

In the morning so soon as we could see the trace, we proceeded on our journey, and had the track until we had compassed the head of a long creek, and there they took into another wood, and we after them, supposing to find some of their dwellings, but we marched through boughs and bushes, and under hills and valleys, which tore our very armor in pieces, and yet could meet with none of them, nor their houses, nor find any fresh water, which we greatly desired, and stood in need of, for we brought neither beer nor water with us, and our victuals was only biscuit and Holland cheese, and a little bottle of aquavitae, so as we were sore athirst. About ten o'clock we came into a deep valley, full of brush, wood-gaile, and long grass, through which we found little paths or tracks, and there we saw a deer, and found springs of fresh water, of which we were heartily glad, and sat us down and drunk our first New England water with as much delight as ever we drunk drink in all our lives.

When we had refreshed ourselves, we directed our course full south, that we might come to the shore, which within a short while after we did, and there made a fire, that they in the ship might see where we were (as we had direction) and so marched on towards this supposed river. And as we went in another valley we found a fine clear pond of fresh water, being about a musket shot broad and twice as long. There grew also many fine vines, and fowl and deer haunted there; there grew much sassafras. From thence we went on, and found much plain ground, about fifty acres, fit for plow, and some signs where the Indians had formerly planted their corn. After this, some thought it best, for nearness of the river, to go down and travel on the sea sands, by which means some of our men were tired, and lagged behind. So we stayed and gathered them up, and struck into the land again, where we found a little path to certain heaps of sand, one whereof was covered with old mats, and had a wooding thing like a mortar whelmed on the top of it, and an earthen pot laid in a little hole at the end thereof. We, musing what it might be, digged and found a bow, and, as we thought, arrows, but they were rotten. We supposed there were many other things, but because we deemed them graves, we put in the bow again and made it up as it was, and left the rest untouched, because we thought it would be odious unto them to ransack their sepulchers.

We went on further and found new stubble, of which they had gotten corn this year, and many walnut trees full of nuts, and great store of strawberries, and some vines. Passing thus a field or two, which were not great, we came to another which had also been new gotten, and there we found where a house had been, and four or five old planks laid together; also we found a great kettle which had been some ship's kettle and brought out of Europe. There was also a heap of sand, made like the former—but it was newly done, we might see how they had paddled it with their hands—which we digged up, and in it we found a little old basket full of fair Indian corn, and digged further and found a fine great new basket full of very fair corn of this year, with some thirty-six goodly ears of corn, some yellow, some red, and others mixed with blue, which was a very goodly sight. The basket was round, and narrow at the top; it held about three or four bushels, which was as much as two of us could lift up from the ground, and was very handsomely and cunningly made. But whilst we were busy about these things, we set our men sentinel in a round ring, all but two or three which digged up the corn. We were in suspense what to do with it and the kettle, and at length, after much consultation, we concluded to take the kettle and as much of the corn as we could carry away with us; and when our shallop came, if we could find any of the people, and come to parley with them, we would give them the kettle again, and satisfy them for their corn. So we took all the ears, and put a good deal of the loose corn in the kettle for two men to bring away on a staff; besides, they that could put any into their pockets filled the same. The rest we buried again, for we were so laden with armor that we could carry no more.

Not far from this place we found the remainder of an old fort, or palisade, which as we conceived had been made by some Christians. This was also hard by that place which we thought had been a river, unto which we went and found it so to be, dividing itself into two arms by a high bank. Standing right by the cut or mouth which came from the sea, that which was next unto us was the less; the other arm was more than twice as big, and not unlike to be a harbor for ships. But whether it be a fresh river, or only an indraught of the sea, we had no time to discover, for we had commandment to be out but two days. Here also we saw two canoes, the one on the one side, the other on the other side; we could not believe it was a canoe, till we came near it. So we returned, leaving the further discovery thereof to our shallop, and came that night back again to the fresh water pond, and there we made our rendezvous that night, making a great fire, and a barricade to windward of us, and kept good watch with three sentinels all night, every one standing when his turn came, while five or six inches of match was burning. It proved a very rainy night.

In the morning we took our kettle and sunk it in the pond, and trimmed our muskets, for few of them would go off because of the wet, and so coasted the wood again to come home, in which we were shrewdly puzzled, and lost our way. As we wandered we came to a tree, where a young sprit was bowed down over a bow, and some acorns strewed underneath. Stephen Hopkins said it had been to catch some deer. So as we were looking at it, William Bradford being in the rear, when he came looked also upon it, and as he went about, it gave a sudden jerk up, and he was immediately caught by the leg. It was a very pretty device, made with a rope of their own making and having a noose as artificially made as any roper in England can make, and as like ours as can be, which we brought away with us. In the end we got out of the wood, and were fallen about a mile too high above the creek, where we saw three bucks, but we had rather have had one of them. We also did spring three couple of partridges, and as we came along by the creek we saw great flocks of wild geese and ducks, but they were very fearful of us. So we marched some while in the woods, some while on the sands, and other while in the water up to the knees, till at length we came near the ship, and then we shot off our pieces, and the long boat came to fetch us.

The Charter of the Colony of New Plymouth

Granted to William Bradford and His Associates: 1629

Note: Some spellings have been adjusted for consistency, and some words have been defined in brackets for clarity.

To all to whom these presents shall come greetinge: Whereas our late sovereign lord king James for the advancement of a collonie and plantacon [plantation] in the cuntry called or knowne by the name of New Englande in America, by his highnes letters pattents under the greate scale of Englande bearinge date at Westminster the third day of November in the eighteenth yeare of his highnes raigne [reign] of England, &c. did give graunte and confirms unto the right honoble Lodowicke late lord duke of Lenox, George late marques of Buckingham, James marques Hamilton, Thomas earle of Arundell, Robert earle of Warwicke and Ferdinando Gorges, Knight, and divers others whose names are expressed in the said letters pattents and their successors that they should be one bodie pollitique and corporate perpeturely consistinge of fourty persons, and that they should have perpetual succession and one common scale to serve for the said body and that they and their successors should be incorporated called and knowne by the name of the Councill

established at Plymouth in the county of Devon for the planting, rulinge orderinge and governinge of New Englande in America, and alsoe of his speciall grace certaine knowledge and more motion did give graunte and confirms unto the said presidents and councill and their successors forever under the reservations limitations and declaracons in the said letters pattents expressed, all that part and portion of the said country called New-England in America scituate [situated], and lyinge and being in breadth from fourty degrees northerly latitude from the equinoctiall line to fourty eight degrees of the said northerly latitude inclusively, and in length of and in all the breadth aforesaide throughout the maine land from sea to sea, together alsoe with all the firms landes soyles grounds creeks inletts havens portes seas rivers islands waters fishinges mynes and mineralls as well royall mines of gold and silver as other mines and mineralls pretious [precious] stones quarries and all and singular the commodities jurisdiccons [jurisdictions] royalties privileges franchises and preheminences [existing contracts] both within the said tracte of lands upon the maine, as also within the said islands and seas adioyninge [adjoining]: To have hold possesse and enjoy all and singuler the foresaid continents landes territories islands hereditaments [inheritable property] and prcints [neighboring] sea waters fishinges with all and all manner their commodities royalties privileges preheminences and profitts that shall arise from thence, with all and singuler their appurtenaces [supplements] and every parte and parcell thereof unto the said councill and their successors and assignee forever: To be holden of his Matie [Majesty], his heirs and successors as of his mannor of East Greenwiche in the county of Kent in free and common soccage [ownership based on a set payment of money or service] and not in capite [stocks or bonds] nor by Knights [military] service yeeldinge and payinge therefore to the said late king's Matie, his heires and successors the fifte parte of the oare [ore] of gold and silver which from tyme [time] to tyme and aft all tymes from the date of the said letters pattents sholbe [should be] there gotten had and obtained for and in respect of all and all manner of duties demands and services whatsoever to be done made and paid unto his said late Matie, his heirs and successors as in and by the said letters pattents amongst sundry other privileges and matters therein contained more fully and at large it doth and may appease. Now knowe ye that the said councill by virtue and authority of his said late Man letters pattents and for and in consideracon that William Bradford and his associatts have for these nine yeares lived in New Englande aforesaid and have there inhabited and planted a towne called by the name of New Plimouth att their own proper costs and charges: And now seeinge that by the speciall providence of God, and their extraordinary care and industry they have increased their plantacon to neere three hundred people, and are uppon all occasions able to relieve any new planters or others his Mats [Majesty's] subjects whoe may fall uppon that coaste; have given granted bargained sould [sold] enfeoffed [given land in exchange for service] allotted assigned and sett over and by these presents doe cleerly and absolutely give graunt bargaine sell alien enfeoffe allots assigne and confirme unto the said William Bradford, his heires associatts and assignee all that part of New-Englande in America aforesaid and tracte and tractes of lande that lye within or betweene a certaine rivolett [stream] or rundlett there commonly called Coahassett alias Conahassett towards the north, and the river commonly called Naragansetts river towards the south; and the great westerne ocean towards the east, and betweene and within a straight line directly extendinge upp into the maine land towards the west from the mouth of the said river called Naragansetts river to the utmost limitts and bounds of a cuntry or place in New Englande called Pokenacutt alias Sowamsett westward, and another like straight line extendinge itself directly from the mouth of the said river called Coahassett alias Conahassett towards the west so farr upp into the maine lande westwardes as the utmost limitts of the said place or cuntry commonly called Pokenacutt alias Sowamsett doe extend, together with one half of the said river called Naragansetts and the said rivolett or rundlett called Coahassett alias Conahassett and all lands rivers waters havens creeks ports fishings fowlings and all hereditaments proffitts comodities and emoluments [wages] whatsoever situate [located] lyinge and beinge or ariseinge within or betweene the said limitts and bounds or any of them. And for as much as they have noe conveniente place-either of tradinge or fishinge within their own precints whereby (after soe longe travell and great paines,) so hopefull a plantacon may subsiste, as alsoe that they may bee incouraged the better to proceed in soe pious a worke which may especially tend to the propagation of religion and the great increase of trade to his Mats realmes, and advancemente of the publique plantacon, the said councill have further given graunted bargained sold enfeoffed allotted assigned and sett over and by these presentes doe cleerely and absolutely give graunte bargaine sell alien enfeoffe allots assigne and confirme unto the said William Bradford his heires associate and assignee all that tracte of lande or parte of New England in America aforesaid which lyeth within or betweene and extendeth itself from the utmost limitts of Cobbiseconte alias Comasee-Conte which adjoineth to the river of Kenebeke alias Kenebekike towards the westerne ocean and a place called the falls att Mequamkike in America aforesaid, and the space of fifteene Englishe miles on each side of the said river commonly called Kenebek river, and all the said river called Kenebek that lies within the said limitts and bounds eastward westward northward or southward laste above mentioned, and all lands grounds soyles [soils] rivers waters fishings hereditaments and proffitts whatsoever situate lyinge and beinge arisinge happeninge or accrueinge, or which shall arise happen or accrue in or within the said limitts and boundes or either of them together with free ingresse egresse and regresse with shipps boates shallopps and other vessels from the sea commonly called the westerne ocean to the said river called Kenebek and from the said river to the said westerne ocean, together with all prerogatives rights royalties jurisdiccons, preveledges franchises liberties and guerenities [guarantees], and alsoe marine liberty with the escheats [giving property back to the Crown] and casualties thereof the Admiralty Jurisdiccon excepted with all the interest right title claime and demande whatsoever which the said councill and their successors now have or ought to have and claime or may have and acquire hereafter in or to any the said porcons [portions] or tractes of land hereby menconed [mentioned] to be graunted, or any the premisses in as free large ample and beneficiall manner to all intents, construccons and purposes whatsoever as the said councill by virtue of his Mats said letters pattents may or can graunte; to have and to horde the said tracte and tractes of lande and all and singular the premisses above menconed to be graunted with their and every of their appurtenances to the said William Bradford his heires associatts and assignee forever, to the only proper and absolute use and behoofe of the said William Bradford his heires associate and assignee forever; Yeeldinge and payinge unto our said soveraigne Lord the Kinge, his heires and successors forever one-fifte parte of the oare of the mines of gold and silver and one other fifte parte thereof to the presidents and councill, which shall be had possessed and obtained within the precints aforesaid for all services and demands whatsoever. And the said councill doe further graunt and agree to and with the said William Bradford his heires associatts and assignee and every of them, his and their Factors agents tenants and servants and all such as hee or they shall send and employ aboute his said particular plantacon, shall and may from tyme to tyme Freely and lawfully goe and returne trade and traffique as well with the Englishe as any of the natines natives] within the precints aforesaid, with liberty of fishinge uppon any parte of the sea coaste and sea shoares of any the seas or islands adjacente and not beinge inhabited or otherwise disposed of by order of the said presidents and councill: also to importe exporte and transports their goods and merchandise aft their wills and pleasures paying only such duty to the Kings Ma [Majesty]

Source: Avalon Project at Yale Law School
http://www.yale.edu/lawweb/avalon/states/mass02.htm

Index